GENOCIDE

Mark Friedman

Heinemann
LIBRARY

Chicago, Illinois

www.capstonepub.com
Visit our website to find out more information about Heinemann-Raintree books.

To order:
☎ Phone 888-454-2279
🖳 Visit www.capstonepub.com
    to browse our catalog and order online.

Edited by Adam Miller, Nick Hunter, and
    Diyan Leake
Designed by Philippa Jenkins
Original illustrations © Capstone Global
    Library Ltd 2012
Picture research by Mica Brancic
Production by Eirian Griffiths and Alison Parsons
Originated by Capstone Global Library Ltd
Printed and bound in the USA by Corporate
Graphics

15 14 13 12 11
10 9 8 7 6 5 4 3 2 1

Library of Congress Cataloging-in-Publication Data
Friedman, Mark, 1963-
  Genocide / Mark Friedman.
     p. cm.—(Hot topics)
  Includes bibliographical references and index.
  ISBN 978-1-4329-6034-6 (hb)—ISBN 978-1-4329-6042-1 (pb) 1. Genocide—History—Juvenile literature. 2. Genocide—Juvenile literature. I. Title.
  HV6322.7.F746 2012
  364.15'10904—dc23
2011017831

Acknowledgments
The author and publisher are grateful to the following for permission to reproduce copyright material: Alamy pp. 20 (© World History Archive), 47 (© Howard Sayer); The Art Archive p. 8 (British Library); Corbis pp. 13 (© Bettmann), 15 (© Bettmann), 17 (© Underwood & Underwood), 26 (Pvt. H. Miller), 29 (© Hulton-Deutsch Collection), 31 (© Bettmann), 34 (Sygma/© Richard Dudman), 36 (Reuters/© Chor Sokunthea), 45 (© Reuters/Fred Ernst), 55 (epa/© Jim Hollander), 57 (In Pictures/© Peter Dench), Corbis/Sygma p. 40 (© Pierre Vauthey)); Getty Images pp. 5 (Daniel Pepper), 7 (The Bridgeman Art Library/Emile Signol), 18 (Time Life Pictures/Timepix/Hugo Jaeger), 22 (National Archives/Handout), 25 (Hulton Archive/Galerie Bilderwelt), 49 (AFP Photo), 53 (Marco Di Lauro); Mary Evans Picture Library p. 28 (Weimar Archive); Reuters p. 43 (Damir Sagolj); Woolaroc Museum p. 10 (Robert Ottakar Lindneux).

Cover photograph of the skeletal remains of some 2,000 victims of the Khmer Rouge regime at a memorial stupa in northwest Cambodia reproduced with permission of Corbis (epa/© Doug Niven).

Every effort has been made to contact copyright holders of any material reproduced in this book. Any omissions will be rectified in subsequent printings if notice is given to the publisher.

CONTENTS

Some words are printed in bold, **like this**. You can find out what they mean by looking in the glossary.

WHAT IS GENOCIDE?

What is genocide? It is an African village where all the people have been murdered, homes burned to the ground. It is an entire religious group ordered to change religion or die. It is a member of one **ethnic** group killing neighbors of a different ethnic group.

Genocide is all of these terrible things. And it is millions of other stories of torture and suffering. This example is from Darfur, a region in the African country of Sudan. When a conflict between Darfur's rebel army and the Sudanese government erupted in 2003, Darfur's villages were attacked by the **militia** (armed non-military force).

Here is how a tribal leader named Jleape remembered the attack on Bardi, a village of 500 people:

"First they dropped bombs from a plane, then the soldiers came. They killed 200 in a few hours, including many children. Then they raped the girls who were left. They threw some bodies on the fire, others into the well."

Why would an army attack a village of 500 innocent people? Why would they wipe out hundreds of little villages? Why would they torture and kill children and elderly citizens?

■ One effect of genocide is that large numbers of people can be forced out of their homes.

In a war, armies fight against enemy armies. In a genocide, the war is against a group of people. A country's ruler or another group wages war on a group of people to **exterminate** them—to get rid of them permanently. Not only are people killed in genocides, but their entire existence is also attacked. Their enemies often attempt to erase all traces of their existence, including their culture and their history.

DEFINING GENOCIDE

In 1948, the **United Nations** wrote a definition for genocide, which at the time was a new word. It said that genocide is the attempt to destroy "a national, ethnic, racial, or religious group" through any of the following acts:

- killing members of the group
- causing serious bodily or mental harm to members of the group
- creating living conditions that will cause the group's destruction (such as starvation)
- preventing births within the group (so its population will not grow)
- moving children to a separate group.

The Crusades

Although we only started using the word *genocide* within the last century, genocide has gone on for many centuries. One example from long ago is the Crusades, a period when armies from the Roman Catholic Church fought a series of battles over the course of more than two centuries.

In the First Crusade, launched in 1095, the Crusaders traveled from Europe to the Holy Land (what is known as Israel today). Muslim leaders and citizens were **expelled** from (forced to leave) Jerusalem. Along the way, the Crusaders also attempted to destroy Jewish communities in Germany.

Why did the Crusaders consider the Jews to be their enemies? Since the time of Jesus Christ, history has seen many periods when Christians have been driven to violence in the belief that Jews were responsible for Jesus's death. There were times when Jews lived alongside Christians in peace, but resentments lay beneath the surface.

As the First Crusade launched, the Crusaders began traveling through Germany on their way to the Holy Land. In city after city, they rounded up the Jews and threatened them with death unless they **converted**. To convert, the Jews would have to abandon the Jewish religion and become Christians. Many Jewish people chose to convert just to stay alive. If they refused, they were murdered. Men, women, and children were slaughtered by the hundreds. In the city of Worms, at least 800 Jews were killed.

DEBATE

Is religion worth fighting and killing for? Many people feel strongly about their religious beliefs. The stronger you believe in something, the more you tend to think that others who disagree are wrong. But does an entire group of people that follows a religion deserve to die because of their beliefs? Do you think people feel this strongly about religion today—that it would be important enough to kill for?

■ Jewish people fell victim to torture and murder during the Crusades.

In some places, the local Christians did their best to save the Jews. In Cologne, for example, the citizens protected the Jews in their homes before the local bishop arranged for them to be sent into hiding in neighboring villages. In most places, however, the townspeople and local church leaders turned the Jews over to the Crusaders and even helped to carry out the torture and killing.

A sense of terror gripped the Jews of Germany. When the Jewish people in a city heard that the Crusaders were about to arrive, many chose to take their own lives rather than suffer at the hands of the Crusaders. People threw themselves into rivers to drown. Parents slit the throats of their own children and then killed themselves rather than allow the Crusaders to murder them.

The Mongol conquests

About a century after the Crusades began in Europe, another period of brutal battles began in Asia. In 1206, Genghis Khan established the Mongol Empire in a region south of China. He quickly launched his armies on a campaign to expand his kingdom. The conquests lasted nearly a century, ending in 1368.

Along the way, the Mongol armies killed thousands in many cities. When a Mongol army arrived at a city, they would order all its citizens to leave their homes and gather outside the city walls. Then, each Mongol soldier would be ordered to kill a certain number of the citizens. Often, they were ordered to provide proof of their killings—they would cut an ear off each person as proof of how many they had killed.

As the Mongol armies moved west, the devastation grew more widespread. In Iran, more than 75 percent of the population was wiped out. In parts of what is now Russia, entire cities were destroyed, their populations eliminated.

The Spanish Inquisition

During the Spanish **Inquisition** (period of investigation), the Christian church **persecuted** people who did not agree with its beliefs. They did not use armies, however. Instead, Church officials and other citizens were given special powers to ask questions, decide guilt, and issue punishments.

The Spanish Inquisition was not the first inquisition in Europe, but it was one of the most brutal and is well known today because it lasted for three centuries, from 1478 into the 1700s. The goal of the Inquisition was to punish **heretics**—people who disagreed with the Church. The Inquisition targeted Christian heretics, Jews, Muslims, and others. **Tribunals** were set up in cities and villages. A tribunal was a type of court.

After a tribunal was established, people were given a grace period in which they could come forward and confess that they were heretics. Or, they would confess that they were secretly practicing another religion. Those who confessed were punished and sometimes tortured. After the grace period ended, the tribunal would identify people they suspected of crimes against the Church. These people were arrested, put on trial, and were usually **executed**. In the 1490s, the Inquisition began expelling non-Christians from Spain.

Genghis Khan

Genghis Khan was a warrior who was born with the name Temüjin in 1162. After bringing together many warring tribes to form the Mongol Empire, Genghis launched a century of brutal war that his sons and other leaders continued after his death in 1227. Through mass murder and stealing in his early years, Genghis created a sense of fear in all who stood in his way. Genghis was so notorious that Adolf Hitler was said to think of him as a role model.

■ This painting shows Genghis Khan fighting the Chinese.

American Indian displacement

In the mid-1800s in the southeastern United States, the U.S. government was anxious to move the American Indians west so that it could take over their lands. Centuries of conflict with American Indians would come to a head in the government's actions against several Indian nations. In 1830, the U.S. Congress passed the Indian Removal Act. This law demanded that American Indians must leave their homes and move west.

■ Many American Indians died from the brutal conditions on the move west.

The law gave Indians the choice of staying. However, if they stayed, they would have to give up their identity as part of their Indian nation. They would have to agree to become citizens of the U.S. state in which they lived.

An important part of any genocide occurs when the ruling power forces a group of people to change its identity. In the Crusades and the Inquisition, the Christian Church forced followers of other religions to convert to Christianity. In 1830, the U.S. government gave American Indians a similar choice: "Get out, or if you stay, become one of us." Some American Indians agreed to stay. Others fought back and refused to go, but it was a battle they could not win. In the end, the U.S. government swept American Indian communities off their lands and forced them to move west.

The Trail of Tears

The **displacement** of the American Indians began in 1831 and continued throughout the 1830s. The government made honest attempts to provide supplies and assistance, but moving tens of thousands of people proved to be a task far beyond what they could handle. Food was in short supply, weather created difficulties, and there were not enough horses, wagons, and boats to carry everyone and their belongings. After surviving the agonizing journey, a Chocktaw chief told a newspaper reporter that he had traveled "a trail of tears and death." This phrase was repeated in newspapers, and the term Trail of Tears took hold as a general description for all Indian removals during this period.

The first step in a removal was that families moved out of their homes and villages and into a nearby **internment camp**. In the overcrowded internment camps, disease spread rapidly, and many people died. Those who survived the camps then had to begin their long journeys across thousands of miles. Many of those miles were traveled on foot, sometimes in brutal winter weather. Men and women, young and old, healthy and ill, all walked in suffering as soldiers prodded them on. Among the Cherokee nation alone, 4,000 people lost their lives. Among all tribes, about 15,000 died on the Trail of Tears.

PATTERNS OF GENOCIDE

In the three examples of genocide we have seen so far, certain patterns emerge. Not every genocide is the same, but most genocides include some of these stages:

- Persecution – when the rulers or government mistreat a group of people. This can occur in many ways, such as spreading lies, stopping the group from earning a living, or taking money or possessions.
- Displacement – when a group of people is expelled from a country
- Public humiliation – when the group is persecuted, tortured, or expelled in plain sight of society
- Selective murder – when certain parts of a population are killed and others do not suffer the same fate

ARMENIA – THE FIRST MODERN GENOCIDE

It would be easy to think of genocide as something evil that happened in our distant past. But the truth is that genocide happens in modern times as well. At the turn of the 20th century, the Ottoman Empire was a centuries-old empire that was struggling to survive. The empire had once stretched from Asia to Europe to Africa, but it had shrunk through the years. By the beginning of the 1900s, the empire was based mainly in and around the area today known as Turkey. Long ago, the empire had conquered the country of Armenia, located just east of Turkey and bordering Russia to the northeast.

The Ottoman Empire in the early 1930s.

■ These Armenian women are building a wall to defend themselves from the Turks.

Why were the Armenians hated?

Armenia's Christian citizens had never fit in well with the largely Muslim Ottoman society and were often targets of persecution. In addition, Ottoman leaders feared that Armenia would eventually gain enough power to become an independent nation. In the last half of the 1800s, Armenian villages were raided frequently by bands of Turks and Kurds—other ethnic groups in the region. Sultan Hamid, ruler of the Ottomans, ordered a series of **massacres**. From 1894 to 1896, between 100,000 and 300,000 Armenians were killed.

Despite the tragedy, this was not the end of the Armenian people. As years passed, their resolve only strengthened, and they continued to be viewed as a threat. However, as Europe marched towards the terrifying reality of World War I, the plight of the Armenians became a low priority in the eyes of other nations.

THE CRIME OF BEING A CULTURE

What crimes do the victims of genocide commit? American Indians wanted to live on the lands they had occupied since the time of their ancestors. Similarly, the Armenians sought fair treatment from the empire that ruled over them. As a whole, these people were simply living their lives in a certain way, in a certain place. They were living their cultures. However, other, more powerful, forces decided that these people's cultures were wrong, or offensive, or that they were simply in the way. And so it became a crime to be a part of that culture.

Armenian genocide

When World War I started in 1914, the Ottoman Empire entered the war on the side of Germany and Austria-Hungary. Opposing them were the **Allied powers**: the United Kingdom, France, and the Russian Empire. When the Turkish (Ottoman) authorities attempted to use Armenian soldiers in the war, the Armenians resisted. Resentment grew quickly, and the Turks began to suspect the Armenians of siding with the Russian enemy.

In February 1915, the Turk military commander stripped all Armenian soldiers of their weapons and made them into laborers. They were put to work building roads, and the conditions in which they worked were brutal. Of the 40,000 men who were forced into this work, very few survived the heat and extreme conditions. Those who did survive were shot.

In the city of Van, an Armenian revolt broke out in April 1915 when the local Turk military demanded the use of 4,000 Armenian soldiers. The Armenians refused to supply that number and fighting began. As more clashes like this popped up, the Turkish rulers realized that to be successful in their war against foreign powers, they had to control the Armenian revolt occurring within their own borders.

The Turks had many reasons to act against the Armenians. One reason was that they wanted to stop the Armenians from disrupting their war effort. But this conflict was also the culmination of centuries of disputes. And so it became a genocide against the Armenian people. The Turkish command made the conscious decision to eliminate the Armenians.

The first step was the removal of Armenian leadership. On a day later called Red Sunday—April 24, 1915—Armenian leaders in the Ottoman capital of Constantinople were arrested and deported. Later they were executed. Soon after, the Turks began to round up any men or older boys who might be able to revolt. Other people who might have been considered leaders were also taken away. Overnight, all of the teachers, artists, or writers in a town would vanish. These Armenians were tied up, taken out of their towns, and shot. In some cases, ordinary Turkish people were allowed to attack the helpless Armenians. The American ambassador to the Ottoman Empire, Henry Morgenthau, later wrote: "When they had traveled five or six hours … a mob of Turkish peasants fell upon [the Armenians] with clubs, hammers, axes, scythes, spades, and saws. Such instruments … caused more agonizing deaths than guns and pistols."

■ Armenian victims are seen in a photo that Ambassador Morgenthau included in his report documenting the genocide.

Death marches

As with other genocides, **deportation** was an important strategy in the Ottoman action against Armenia. For the American Indians of the southeastern United States, the destination was "Indian Territory" west of the Mississippi River. For the Armenians, there was no real destination. They were told they were going to be moved out of danger from the war, but this was a lie. They were forced to walk hundreds of miles across rough, open terrain, through mountains, and into the desert of Deir ez-Zor in Syria. Those who did not die from exhaustion, hunger, or disease were treated brutally. Some were beaten. Some were stripped of their clothes and forced to walk in the desert sun without any protection or any water. Large groups of people were forced into lakes to drown. Some were simply murdered: shot, hung, or burned to death.

At the beginning of the war, about two million Armenians lived in the Ottoman Empire. By the end of the war in 1918, one million of those had been killed in the genocide, and at least another half-million escaped or were deported. But it wasn't just the people themselves that the Turks attempted to exterminate. They also tried to destroy the very memory of those people. They tore down Armenian churches and destroyed artwork, documents, and libraries. A 3,000-year-old culture was reduced to rubble. The Turks attempted to make it seem as though Armenia had never existed.

Joseph Kalajian was a child during the Armenian genocide. This is his memory.

"My mother was holding my hand. We were being deported. We walked and walked. Within an hour we saw the bodies of the killed people rotting under the sun. I was terribly afraid. I held my nose from the horrible odor and closed my eyes so I could not see."

The world reacts

The outside world knew that Armenians were being persecuted. A headline in the *New York Times* on December 15, 1915 stated: "Millions Armenians Killed or in Exile … Policy of Extermination." Newspapers around the world repeated these reports, and eventually the world saw photographs: visual proof of the **atrocities**. Photography was a relatively new invention, and Armenia was the first genocide in history to be documented with photos as proof of the events. Still, to this day, some people in Turkey continue to deny that the genocide ever happened, or they defend the deportations as a necessary step in Turkey's security during the war.

Some people attempt to erase the guilt of the past by denying that genocides occurred. In Turkey, Germany, and other countries, some people speak out and argue that genocides never occurred. They claim that the stories are lies, the photos are fakes, and the estimated numbers of victims are overblown. Some governments try to stop these people from spreading these thoughts. Do you think people should be free to speak and write about such beliefs in public? Should governments have the right to stop the free speech of genocide-deniers?

After the war, the United States and the United Kingdom led an effort to prosecute the Turkish leaders who carried out the genocide. These leaders all escaped into Germany. Although a trial was held and convictions were handed down, the criminals were never caught or punished.

The Allied powers expressed outrage over the genocide and discussed the need to support the surviving Armenians. It was the first time that world leaders had reacted in this way to a genocide. But these feelings failed to become real assistance for Armenia. No programs were put into place to provide aid. And the United States, the United Kingdom, and other countries failed to support the surviving Armenians when they again fell under attack in Turkey after the war. Eventually, a small Armenian state was established within the **Soviet Union**, while no Armenians were living in Turkey.

■ On "death marches," Armenians were often forced to walk until they died.

THE HOLOCAUST

If humanity learned anything from the Armenian genocide, those lessons were quickly forgotten. Just a decade later, the patterns leading to genocide unfolded once again, this time in Germany. The victims? Primarily, the Jewish people, but other minorities were targeted, too. This next episode of human cruelty would nearly wipe the Jewish people off the map in Europe. In Hebrew, this period came to be called HaShoah or Shoah, which means "a calamity" or "great destruction." In English, a similar word meaning "destruction by fire" was used: *holocaust*.

■ Adolf Hitler rose to power by inspiring the German people and by creating the idea that Jews and other minorities were enemies living among them.

Hitler's rise to power

In the late 1920s, Adolf Hitler and his Nazi party began to rise to power in Germany. Hitler spoke of ridding Germany of the "aliens" who were living among them. These were cultural groups such as gypsies, political groups such as liberals, homosexuals, the physically or mentally impaired, and—especially—the Jews.

Hitler seized control in 1933. He openly discussed his ideas for making Germany a land of a single race—an "**Aryan**" race of pure Germans. To preserve Aryan purity, Hitler said that other "alien" races must be eliminated, setting the stage for a genocide. An important moment at the start of any genocide occurs when a community or nation believes the idea of "us against them."

Soon after Hitler became Chancellor of Germany, the Nazis established laws that restricted the rights of "alien" groups. One law forced sterilization on anyone thought to have genetic defects. Sterilization is a medical procedure that makes a person unable to have babies. The Nazis hoped to kill off the next generation of Jews before they could be born.

CASE STUDY

The Jews as scapegoats

The Jews of Germany in the 1930s suffered from similar treatment as did Jewish communities of the past. The Jews were made into scapegoats—convenient targets to blame for all of the ills of a society. Because the Jewish faith required Jewish people to live by a different set of rules and follow a different diet, the larger non-Jewish population often feared and resented the Jews' differences. So, if an unexplained calamity struck a community, the Jews were easy targets for blame. If a plague entered the community, Jews might be accused of poisoning the water in wells. If a child went missing, Jews might be blamed for kidnapping the child. In 1930s Germany, many Jewish people were involved in banking and finance. So, when an economic depression affected many nations including Germany, the Jews were blamed once again. In many genocides, a particular religious or ethnic group is made a scapegoat. The society invents reasons to blame the group for things that are not their fault.

Separating the Jews from society

In September 1935, the Nazis passed the Nuremberg Laws, which officially separated the Jews from German society. The laws stated that Jews could not marry or have sexual relations with Germans. In 1938, more **anti-Semitic** laws were passed. Jews were stopped from owning certain kinds of businesses. They had to apply for identity cards. Jewish doctors were banned from practicing medicine. Jews could no longer be lawyers. Such laws are typical steps in the build-up to a genocide.

PROPAGANDA

To destroy the Jews, Hitler needed the cooperation of the German people. Resistance from ordinary citizens could have prevented his plan, so Hitler encouraged them to fear and hate the Jews.

The Nazis seized control of the media and created information that was either a twisted version of truth or outright lies. This manipulation of media messages is called **propaganda**. Through newspaper articles, posters, books, and films, the Nazis portrayed Jews as greedy, money-grubbing monsters. Germans were told that Jews were an inferior race and were physically flawed. The Nazi propaganda also glorified the superior Aryan race.

Even children's books were produced that cast Jews as monsters with exaggerated features such as hooked noses, large ears, and filthy beards. A German children's book, *Money Is the God of the Jews*, included the following lines that a mother tells her child: "Child, you must realize … The Jew is not a person like us. The Jew is a Devil … The God of the Jews is gold. There is no crime he would not commit to get it … And with this money he would make us all slaves and destroy us."

■ This German propaganda cartoon shows a Jewish person as greedy.

Soon enough, outright violence against Jews exploded. On November 9, 1938, mobs of Germans ran through the streets in many German cities and towns, breaking windows, burning homes and businesses, beating up and murdering Jews. On this "Night of Broken Glass"—*Kristallnacht*—a savage brand of persecution of the Jews came out into the open.

World War II begins

When Germany invaded Poland in September 1939 to begin World War II, the lives of Jews across Eastern Europe were thrown into chaos. Hitler joined with Italy and several other countries in Europe to form the **Axis powers**. They marched into one country after another, placing about 9.5 million Jews across Europe under Hitler's power.

■ This map shows the countries that Germany had invaded by 1942.

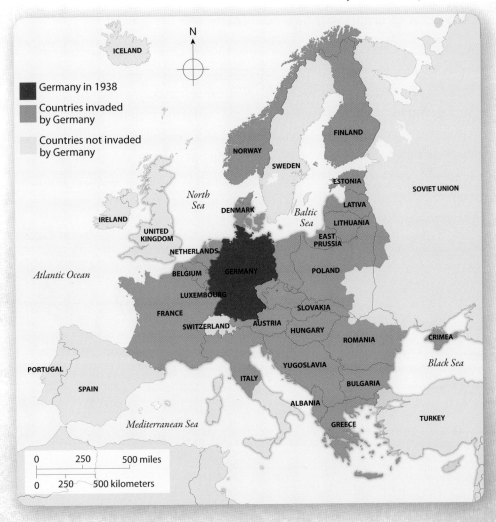

Throughout the 1930s, the Nazis built **concentration camps** in Germany to hold prisoners who were arrested and deported for various crimes. As the war progressed, the Nazis built more concentration camps throughout the countries they occupied. Some sources say that, by the end of the war in 1945, the Nazis had operated 15,000 camps across Europe.

In September 1941, Hitler began ridding Germany of Jews. After years of separating Jews from society in the *minds* of Germans, the Jews were now being separated *physically*. Jews were rounded up and deported to concentration camps in vast numbers. Many were also sent to ghettos— restricted areas of a city where the Jews were forced to live in terrible conditions. The city of Warsaw, Poland, was the site of a massive ghetto of 400,000 Jews. Whether in ghettos or concentration camps, Jews were prisoners and treated with cruelty. Food was scarce, living conditions were cramped, and disease was rampant. Death lurked everywhere.

Meanwhile, as the German army advanced across Europe, the Nazis treated each country's Jews with swift, deadly cruelty. In the German-occupied Soviet Union, squads of Nazi soldiers called **Einsatzgruppen** invaded Jewish neighborhoods, captured the Jews, and separated the men from the women. The able-bodied men were imprisoned and sent to work in camps. The women, children, and elderly men were taken out of town, stripped naked, and murdered. Soldiers would line them up on the side of a pit and shoot them so the bodies would fall into the pit. Often, the prisoners themselves would be forced to dig the pit before being murdered.

■ Jewish people were forced out of their homes by Nazi soldiers.

The Nazis' many victims

Although Jews formed the majority of the Nazi's victims, they were not the only targets. During the Holocaust, the Nazis also killed millions of others whom they saw as weak or impure, such as the mentally ill or physically handicapped. They also targeted the Romani people (known as gypsies), another ethnic group whose clans lived throughout Eastern Europe. They killed anyone who could be proved to think differently – **intellectuals** and **communists** who supported political ideas different from the Nazis. Also, citizens and soldiers of the countries conquered by Germany were murdered in large numbers, particularly in Poland and the Soviet Union.

In total, the Nazis murdered about 6 million Jews, but overall, more than 17 million people died at the hands of the Nazis. However, it was the Jews who were a primary focus of Nazi hatred. It was the Jews whom the Nazis most wished to wipe out of existence.

CASE STUDY

Stalin: Ally or villain?

During World War II, the United Kingdom, the United States, and France found themselves allied with the Soviet Union, the massive communist nation of Eastern Europe. The Soviet Union, however, was an uneasy ally. Joseph Stalin, the Soviet leader, had treated Soviet citizens with a cruelty that rivaled Hitler's. Just a decade earlier, Stalin had attempted to solve a long-standing dispute with neighboring Ukraine by starving its population. Although the full truth of the Ukrainian Holodomor (which means "death by hunger") was not known for decades, between 6 and 7 million Ukrainians starved in 1932–33 because Stalin withheld food from them. Throughout his reign, Stalin ordered mass deaths of many other enemies, within and beyond the Soviet Union.

Death camps

Killing a massive number of people one by one, face to face, was messy, distressing to the soldiers, and inefficient. The Nazis looked for newer ways of killing larger numbers of people more quickly. Eventually, the Nazis built an even larger system for killing massive numbers of people—the **death camps**.

The idea of death camps was part of the Nazi's "Final Solution," a conscious, planned strategy for wiping out the Jewish population. Planning for the first death camp, Auschwitz in Poland, began in early 1940, and by September 1941, Nazis were testing the use of a substance called Zyklon B at Auschwitz. It proved to be an extremely effective poison. Zyklon B pellets produced a gas called cyanide, which kills people almost instantly when inhaled.

The Holocaust was different as compared to other genocides because of the interest the Nazis took in improving the speed and efficiency of the killings. The Turks, for instance, led Armenians on long and torturous death marches. The Nazis wanted to kill enormous numbers of people much more quickly.

The Nazis built death camps that were factories in which murder could be accomplished at great speed. They deliberately built them on railway lines (or built rail tracks leading to the camps) so that prisoners could be transported directly to the camps. These camps were in operation from 1942 to the end of World War II in 1945.

Estimated number of deaths at death camps

Place	Number of deaths
Auschwitz–Birkenau (Poland)	1,100,000
Belzec (Poland)	434,000
Chelmno (Poland)	152,000
Jasenovac (Croatia)	80,000
Majdank (Poland)	47,000
Maly Trostenets (Belarus)	65,000
Sajmiste (Serbia)	100,000
Sobibor (Poland)	167,000
Treblinka (Poland)	870,000
Warsaw (Poland)	200,000

CASE STUDY

Auschwitz–Birkenau

In September 1942, mass killings commenced at Auschwitz, in Poland. It was the largest and most effective camp built by the Nazis. Auschwitz was actually a network of several camps built closely together, and they were linked to Birkenau, a prison camp. The operation of Auschwitz was similar to the operation of many other death camps. Jews were transported to the camp by train, forced out of the trains by armed guards, and separated immediately into those who were fit for work and those who were not. Those who could not work—mostly women, children, and elderly men—were led to a building where they were told to shower. All the people were forced to undress and move into a large room equipped with showerheads, which were fake. Once inside, the doors were locked, and a guard on the roof would drop Zyklon B pellets into the room, releasing the poisonous gas. In a matter of minutes, everyone in the room was dead. Workers (who were actually prisoners of the camp, not Nazi guards) then entered the room, hauled out the bodies, and brought them to a crematorium—massive ovens where the bodies were burned.

■ Terrified Jewish prisoners arrived by train at Auschwitz.

Witnesses, bystanders

One question that every citizen must grapple with is how he or she would act if one's own government were to commit crimes such as those committed by the Nazis. We must remember that Nazi propaganda led Germans to believe that Jews were being deported to live in occupied territories to the East. And through propaganda, the Nazis had convinced many Germans that the Jews were an alien race who must be removed.

Consider the few options open to someone who objected to the Nazis' actions. To speak out or act against the Nazis could have easily led to one's own deportation or death. Yet many people did resist the Nazis. In Denmark, for example, the Danish people worked against the Nazis and successfully transported about 8,000 Jews safely to Sweden. In France, the town of Le Chambon defied the Nazis and saved the lives of approximately 5,000 Jews. Throughout Europe and within Germany, there were examples of individuals who summoned the courage to smuggle money, food, passports, weapons, or other necessities to Jews. Perhaps the most famous story is that of Miep Geis and other Dutch citizens who risked their lives to provide supplies to Anne Frank, her family, and other Jews who hid in an Amsterdam attic for two years.

When judging whether German citizens were guilty of being bystanders, we must also remember that the mass murders in the death camps were usually committed out of sight from the public. In the remote towns in Poland, where the death camps were operating, local peasants may have had an idea of what was going on behind the camp walls. However, if they had objected (and many did not), they would have been powerless to do anything about it.

■ The world was shocked to view photos and films of death camp survivors.

CASE STUDY

Christa M

Christa M was a teenage girl living near Munich, Germany, during the war. One day she was walking down a road, returning from buying cheese. She encountered a group of prisoners being transported out of a concentration camp.

"My God, they were skeletons, I mean skeletons. I'll never forget the eyes. The eyes were three times the size because there were no more faces … and skeleton hands. And I see all these people and the ones that were against the wall, they couldn't even walk. They could not walk … So I immediately went towards them … I started opening my rucksack and the minute I reached in and got the first piece, these people came literally crawling, if you can imagine crawling, as much as they could, on hands and knees, towards you. Just looked at you … So I gave the cheese out … [And a Nazi guard] … he's got the big German shepherd and he screamed at me … 'If you give those bastards one more piece of whatever you got there,' he said, 'I'm going to make you join them.' … And I started running."

WHAT WOULD YOU DO?

No genocide can be carried out invisibly or silently. People do see and hear. With any genocide, witnesses are faced with three choices:

1. join the movement and participate in the atrocity
2. risk death by working against the criminals, or
3. do nothing and be a bystander.

None of the three is an easy choice. What would you do? Do you think you could gather the courage to fight a ruling force, even if it would mean risking punishment or death?

CASE STUDY

The Nuremberg Trials

In the immediate aftermath of the Holocaust, the Allies made certain that the truth would come to light and that justice would be served. The Allies captured Nazi leaders, but Hitler and several members of his inner circle had committed suicide in the final days of the war. Many key figures who had given orders in the Holocaust could not be tried. Still, 24 other powerful Nazis were put on trial beginning in November 1945. The trials were called the Nuremberg Trials, as they were held in the German city of Nuremberg. A group of judges from the United Kingdom, France, the Soviet Union, and the United States was selected.

■ Nazis on trial at Nuremberg with armed guards behind them.

Holding all individuals responsible

The 1945 trials were just the first phase of the Nuremberg Trials. From 1946 to 1948, the United States held additional trials at Nuremberg to dig deeper and assign guilt and responsibility to those who worked with, and for, the Nazis. There was a trial of doctors who had performed gruesome medical experiments on prisoners, a trial of lawyers and judges who upheld the racial laws created by the Nazis, an Einsatzgruppen trial for soldiers in the brutal death squads that terrorized Eastern Europe, and many others. A total of 142 people were convicted, and 12 were executed.

The purpose of the trials was clear: the Allies intended to place blame and force the world to recognize that many people (not just Hitler) were responsible for these atrocities. Germany could not explain it away by claiming they were ruled by a madman in Hitler. Germans were not allowed to wriggle off the hook by claiming, "I was just following orders." The Nuremberg Trials attempted to show the world that a genocide is not a machine that cannot be controlled. Rather, genocide is the result of conscious, intentional actions. These actions are committed by individuals who have the ability to decide whether to act or not. The Allies' greatest fear was that, if the perpetrators were not blamed and punished, another genocide could easily occur.

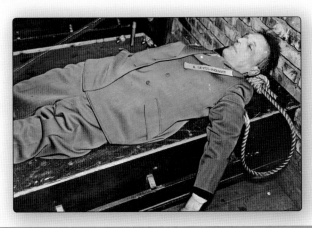

■ Nazi war criminal Arthur Seyss-Inquart, after execution at Nuremberg. He served as Hitler's governor in Austria.

Among those on trial at Nuremberg were Herman Göring, long-time second in command behind Hitler; Rudolf Hess, Secretary of the Nazi Party and Hitler's third in command for several years; Wilhelm Frick, Minister of the Interior and the man who wrote the Nuremberg Laws; and Albert Speer, an architect and Minister of Armaments who used slave labor to create weapons for the Nazis, and who actually apologized during his trial. In the end, the judges sentenced 12 of the 24 to death by hanging. Three were acquitted (found not guilty), and the rest were sent to prison.

Who is to blame?

Is it possible to punish every single individual who takes part in a genocide? Only about 200 people were put on trial in Germany. Thousands of others also acted in support of the Nazis. The world continues to struggle with how to hand out punishment for a crime so large. It is easy to execute the true leaders of a genocide, but how do you punish all of the followers?

The Allied lawyers and judges made sure that the Nuremberg Trials were seen and heard around the world. With both the Nuremberg Trials and the establishment of the United Nations, world leaders hoped to prevent more genocides. Despite these efforts, it appears that lessons were not learned. Almost immediately after the Holocaust, more innocent people in other lands met a similar fate.

DEBATE

Do you think the Nuremberg Trials went far enough? There were thousands of guards, officers, and others who worked at concentration camps and death camps and sent people to their deaths. Do you think more people should have been put on trial? Do you think that a German person should have been let off the hook if he defended himself by saying "I was just following orders"?

INVENTING THE TERM GENOCIDE

At the Nuremberg Trials, the word *genocide* was first heard in an international court. The term was the invention of a Jewish Polish lawyer named Raphael Lemkin.

Born in 1900, Lemkin had grown up reading about history and was both fascinated and appalled by accounts of mass killing in the past, including the massacres of the Mongol Empire and the Armenian genocide that took place when he was a teenager. When Lemkin grew up, he became a lawyer.

■ Raphael Lemkin.

The Nazis invaded Poland in 1939, and Lemkin made a narrow escape to freedom in Sweden.

During this time, he continued to study and write about his obsession with mass killings and his outrage that the perpetrators were never punished adequately. As he wrote about the topic, he eventually devised a new word to describe these acts: *genocide*. The word combines the Greek *genos*, which means "race," "group," or "tribe," with the Latin *−cide*, which means "killing."

At the Nuremberg Trials, Lemkin tried to convince the lawyers that the Nazis should have been put on trial for genocide. Some listened to him, and the term genocide was used during the trial, but it was not a part of the official charges.

Lemkin then traveled to New York to work with leaders who were forming the United Nations. The United Nations enthusiastically adopted Lemkin's ideas about genocide, which formed the basis for current international laws concerning such crimes. (See page 5 for a list of crimes that the United Nations counts as genocide.)

CAMBODIA 1975–1978

Immediately following World War II, the Allies who fought together suffered a split. The communist Soviet Union was an ally to the United Kingdom, the United States, and other countries during the war. But as soon as the war ended, the Soviets became more of an enemy. Their communist political philosophy stood at odds with **democracy**. In the 1950s, Western nations feared the spread of communism into other countries. The Soviets and Americans settled into a "cold" war—it was called the "cold" war because it never got "hot" with direct fighting.

The United States took an active role in putting down the rise of Soviet-influenced communist power in other countries. Two Asian nations that experienced a growing communist presence were Vietnam and Cambodia. In the Vietnam War (1954–75), the United States provided money and military support to South Vietnam against the communist North Vietnamese. U.S. planes also bombed communist operations in neighboring Cambodia. As the war progressed, it became clear that the North Vietnamese would win, which only boosted the communist movement in Cambodia. These communists in Cambodia were called the Khmer Rouge.

Pol Pot, the leader of the Khmer Rouge, had spent years in the country's rural lands, winning the support of farmers and other workers who resented how they were being treated by the ruling Cambodian government. With this support, Pol Pot and the Khmer Rouge seized control of Cambodia when they captured the capital city of Phnom Penh on April 17, 1975.

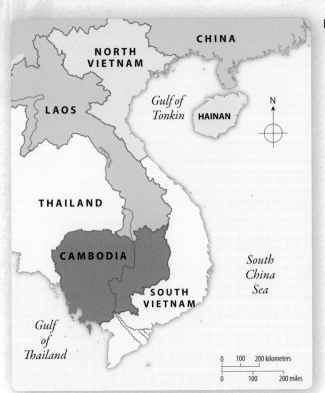

The region of Southeast Asia in 1975.

Removing classes, removing people

At the heart of the communist philosophy is the idea that there should be no classes that separate people. All citizens should have equal ownership of all property, and so it is wrong for an upper class to own more than a lower class. The Khmer Rouge believed that peasants living in rural areas were the ideal Cambodian citizens. Called *neak moultanh*, or "base people," they were not educated, had no possessions, and knew how to work to make their own food and homes. The Cambodians who lived in cities were the complete opposite. These *neak thmei*, or "new people," were educated. They had jobs and bought material things such as cars and furniture and nice clothes.

As soon as he took control of Cambodia, Pol Pot introduced a dramatic set of changes aimed at breaking down class differences. Pol Pot tried to force the "new people" to become "base people." And he attempted to do this almost overnight.

The first step was to force Cambodians out of the cities and into the countryside. They were told lies about U.S. planes coming to bomb them, so they fled their homes in fear. They did not realize that they were being deported.

33

As we now know from past genocides, two of the early key stages in a genocide are the labeling of different types of people and, then, displacement. Before deporting Jews, the Nazis created laws and used propaganda to make people believe that Jews were different from everyone else. They even went as far as forcing Jews to wear a yellow Star of David on their clothing so that everyone would know who they were.

A strangely similar "us and them" movement was at work in Cambodia. Even though Pol Pot's apparent goal was to blend all people into one class, the process started by labeling the classes. He emphasized the divisions in Cambodian society. When the government or ruler of a country creates these differences, it becomes easier for the rest of the nation to believe that one group is less worthy, less human. If one group believes the other is less than human, the groundwork has been laid for genocide.

Pol Pot turned the city people into true foreigners, cast adrift in their own country. Once they reached the countryside, these "new people" were forced into camps where the communists attempted to reeducate them. They were told that their family structures were to change. Children could no longer call their parents "mother" or "father." Individual clothing was banned: everyone wore the same kind of clothes to appear equal.

■ Pol Pot, around September 1978.

CASE STUDY

Communist leadership

In the first three-fourths of the 20th century, communism spread throughout the world. Strong communist regimes rose up and took control of many countries. The Soviet Union and China were the two largest communist nations, and communism spread throughout Asia (North Korea, Vietnam, Cambodia), Europe (East Germany, Yugoslavia, Poland, etc.), Africa (Ethiopia, Somalia, Angola, etc.), and Latin America (Cuba). Often, a communist government was ruled by a single leader who had complete power over the people (such as Pol Pot in Cambodia or Stalin in the Soviet Union). While not all communist leaders have launched genocides, the **human rights** record of most communist leaders is poor. Citizens who object to the ruler are punished severely, and minority or religious groups are often persecuted.

In the 1990s, several communist regimes crumbled as the Soviet Union and others were replaced by democracies. Yet, communism still rules in China and several other nations today.

Persecution

In addition to their attempted merging of the "new" and "base" people, the Khmer Rouge went about changing Cambodian society in other, more brutal ways. The Khmer Rouge murdered minorities, foreigners, and anyone seen as an outsider. Anyone who might bring outside ideas into the country was killed. A minority group called the Cham was persecuted—about half of their population of one million was killed. People who belonged to minority religions—mainly Christians and Muslims—were killed or deported.

Buddhism was the dominant religion in Cambodia, but in the early stages of the revolution, Pol Pot wished to change rather than kill the majority of Cambodians. So, instead of killing Buddhists, he ordered the deaths of Buddhist monks, the leaders of the religion. Historians estimate that approximately 60,000 of the Buddhist monks in Cambodia were slaughtered.

The killing fields

In the vast rural fields beyond Phnom Penh, about 20,000 different mass graves were dug. After Cambodian prisoners were transported to these fields, they were murdered in a particularly brutal way. To save bullets for the military, soldiers killed their prisoners with other weapons, such as axes, iron bars, or gardening hoes. They became known as the "killing fields." More than 1.3 million people were discarded there.

■ Skulls of victims are on display at a memorial to the killing fields in Kampong Cham province, 78 miles (125 kilometers) east of Phnom Penh, Cambodia.

CASE STUDY

Tuol Sleng

In Phnom Penh there was a building, known as Tuol Sleng Center, where suspected enemies of the party were taken for questioning and often torture. This former high school had been turned into a prison where 17,000 people passed through from 1975 to 1979. Incredibly, just 7 of those 17,000 survived.

At Tuol Sleng, prisoners were tortured to the point that they eventually confessed to the crimes of which they were accused. When they confessed, the prisoners were taken out of the center, transported to a rural area outside of the city, and executed. Tuol Sleng was just one such center in Cambodia.

Starvation

The final stage of Pol Pot's reign was marked by starvation. Mass starvation is a common occurrence in many genocides. When a society is disrupted to such a degree as to allow genocide to occur, the society may experience a basic breakdown in ordinary processes. If production of food is interrupted, a huge number of people already living in poverty will quickly slip into starvation. The city people had no skills in farming, and the Khmer Rouge did not know how to organize a farming system. Cambodia experienced a severe decline in crop production. Pol Pot used this **famine** to kill off more groups of opponents. He cut their food rations, and this led to widespread death from starvation.

The Cambodian genocide came to an end in 1979 when a simmering battle with Vietnam resulted in the Vietnamese invading Cambodia and expelling Pol Pot. Approximately 1.7 million people were killed in the genocide, about 25 percent of the country's population. Historians debate whether the gruesome events in Cambodia actually add up to a true genocide. Unlike other genocides, there did not seem to be a single ethnic or political group that Pol Pot targeted. Instead, he caused the deaths of millions from many different groups. Some historians agree that this fact may make Pol Pot the most evil perpetrator of all. In Cambodia, the people's leader made war on the people themselves, with no single enemy in mind.

"ETHNIC CLEANSING" IN THE FORMER YUGOSLAVIA

As the 20th century progressed, video cameras, satellite technology, and airplane travel made it easier for people to witness events happening anywhere in the world. Unfortunately, the idea that "the world is watching" did not prevent genocide from happening during the last quarter of the 20th century.

Breakup of Yugoslavia

In the years after World War II, Yugoslavia was a communist republic made up of six regions: Serbia, Croatia, Bosnia and Herzegovina (also called just Bosnia), Slovenia, Montenegro, and Macedonia. After its ruler, Josip Tito, died in 1980, Yugoslavia was rocked by instability. Tensions rose between ethnic groups. Then, in 1991, the Soviet Union collapsed. This led to the fall of communist governments across Europe.

In some cases, democratic governments rose up in peaceful transitions of power. However, the breakup of the Yugoslavian republics was anything but peaceful. A four-year war began in 1991 when Serbia invaded Croatia. The following year, ethnically mixed Bosnia fell into war when Bosnian Serbs attacked other Bosnians during a peaceful rally in the capital city of Sarajevo.

■ Yugoslavia broke up into six countries in the 1990s.

The Bosnian Serbs wanted to set up their own state within Bosnia, but, in this small region, such a state would be difficult to establish. Bosnia was home to a rich mix of ethnicities—Muslims, Serbs, Croats, Roma (gypsies), Jews, and Albanians. People from these groups lived together in mixed neighborhoods. To carve out their own state, the Bosnian Serb army attempted to wipe out any non-Serbs in the region, particularly the Muslims. Here, the genocide began. Concentration camps were built where thousands of prisoners were held, tortured, and starved. Innocent people were rounded up and executed.

DEBATE

Many genocides are based on hatred between ethnic groups who live as neighbors, as in the former Yugoslavia. Is it possible for groups of different religions or ethnicities to live in peace? Where you live, do you know of tensions between ethnic or religious groups? Have these differences ever become violent?

CASE STUDY

Omarska

In the Bosnian mining village of Omarska, the Bosnian Serbs built a prison camp where thousands of Muslim and Croat prisoners were sent. At the camp, prisoners lived in appalling conditions with little food. Prisoners were tortured mercilessly, and large numbers of women were raped. Omarska became the most notorious concentration camp of the Bosnian conflict.

In 2001, a United Nations tribunal convicted five Bosnian Serbs for their actions in the camp. Four of the five were guards. The fifth, Zoran Zigic, was not even a guard. He was a local taxi driver who repeatedly visited the camp because he enjoyed participating in the humiliation and torture of the prisoners.

■ Television cameras captured the plight of starving prisoners in the Omarska prison camp.

Ethnic cleansing

In this genocide, the killing and torture was not just committed by the Bosnian Serbs. Bosnian Croats and Muslims managed to fight back. In areas where they had greater numbers and control, they too used torture and murder to eliminate Serbs. But the Bosnian Serbs were backed by the massive Serb army, and they carried out a far greater number of atrocities.

In the Bosnian conflict, a new term entered the language: **ethnic cleansing**. The clear intent of the warring sides was to carve out a region for one's own ethnic group and to scrub the landscape clean of other ethnic groups. Bosnia may have been the first genocide in which "ethnic cleansing" was used as a label, but the practice of ethnic cleansing has been used in many other genocides throughout history.

CASE STUDY

Ethnic cleansing in Iraq

Ethnic cleansing has been practiced by many different rulers to remove ethnic groups living within their borders. For instance, in 1988, Iraq's ruler, Saddam Hussein, attempted to "clean" northern Iraq of the Kurds, an ethnic group that had lived there for centuries. Saddam attacked the Kurds, not only with guns and bombs, but he also used **chemical weapons**. Saddam's attacks on the Kurds, among many other factors, led the United Kingdom, the United States, and other nations to join together to go to war against Iraq and, ultimately, remove Saddam Hussein from power.

Help from the outside world

Unlike most other genocides, the events in Bosnia did not take place out of sight from the outside world. Although the extent of the mass killings would be revealed later, leaders of other nations knew that a human tragedy was unfolding in Bosnia. Nevertheless, the world's response proved to be ineffective. None of the world's superpowers (such as the United States or the Soviet Union) stepped in with military aid, as they had done and would continue to do in other conflicts. NATO (a group of countries called the North Atlantic Treaty Organization) planes were used to engage the Serbian jets that were bombing Bosnia.

The United Nations sent "peacekeeping forces" into the region to protect innocent people. These armies operate under the United Nations pledge to keep peace, and not make war. In Bosnia and in other conflicts, the United Nations peacekeepers have been sent in—not to fight for one side or the other— but to defend innocent victims. This can be a difficult position for an army. For many reasons, the United Nations peacekeepers proved ill-equipped to make a significant impact on the Bosnian conflict.

Srebrenica

A key example of the United Nations' difficulties was the slaughter of Srebrenica. As terror reigned throughout Bosnia, Muslims and other refugees fled their homes and sought safety elsewhere. Tens of thousands flooded the streets of the Bosnian city of Srebrenica, which was not fully controlled by the Bosnian Serbs.

In 1993, the United Nations installed a protection force unit of 850 soldiers there to protect the refugees. The United Nations declared that Srebrenica was a safe zone and that refugees should be allowed to exist there in peace. As time passed, however, complaints arose that the United Nations soldiers were doing little to protect them. By 1995, the United Nations force had dwindled to 450, and they were short on supplies and weapons. The Bosnian Serbs were bearing down on Srebrenica, and in July 1995 the army moved in and conquered the city.

In the following week, the single greatest massacre in Europe since World War II took place in Srebrenica. Although many women, children, and elderly people were killed in the siege, the Serbs targeted Bosnian men and teenage boys in particular. Clearly, their intent was to sap the enemy of its ability to build an army. The Serb army mapped out specific plans for where to carry out the executions and dispose of the bodies. Beginning on July 13, the Bosnian males were separated from their families, placed on trucks, and driven to the execution points. Their hands were tied behind their backs, and they were gunned down. In the span of about one week, 8,000 men and boys were killed.

CASE STUDY

Ron Haviv

Ron Haviv was a photojournalist who managed to get permission from the Serbian army to take photographs during the Serb advance into Bosnia. He recalls:

> The Serbian soldiers brought out another person … And he put his arms up and basically looked at me as if I was probably the only person that could save him, which, probably in his mind, I was, but unfortunately there wasn't really anything I could do. They brought him to the headquarters, and as I was standing there I heard a great crash, and I looked up and out of a second floor window, this man came flying out and landed at my feet. And amazingly, he survived the fall and they came over … And they started kicking him and beating him and then dragged him back into the home.
>
> I had to make sure there was a document, that there had to be evidence of this crime, of what was happening. And that, I think, gave me the courage to try to take those photographs. I was shaking, for sure, when I was doing it because I realized how precarious everything was, but I really thought it was unbelievably important to be able to have the world see what happened.

■ Ron Haviv has won awards for his photos of conflicts around the world.

The end and aftermath

The massacre of Srebrenica was so monumental that the outside world finally took decisive action to end the Bosnian conflict. Backed by the United States, the NATO air force launched a massive bombing mission in August 1995. This, combined with Croat and Muslim forces on the ground, drove the Serbs back toward their border.

Two months later, the United States and Russia brought the leaders of Serbia, Croatia, and Bosnia to Dayton, Ohio for a peace conference. The treaty reached there, called the Dayton Peace Agreement, was signed in Paris on December 14, 1995.

Seven years later, Slobodan Milošević, the president of Serbia who signed that peace treaty, was put on trial by a United Nations war tribunal. At the time, Milošević's Serbia was involved in yet another war in Kosovo, but he stood trial for war crimes, crimes against humanity, and the genocide at Srebrenica.

Using the United Nations' definition of genocide, the tragedy at Srebrenica was the only single event that truly qualified. Senior officials from other sides in the wars were also put on trial, as criminal cruelty had been displayed by countries other than Serbia.

Milošević's trial continued into 2006, but he died in his prison cell of an apparent heart attack before a verdict could be reached. Committed to rooting out all responsible individuals, the United Nations' tribunals continue to investigate and pursue war criminals.

In July 2008, Radovan Karadžić was hunted down and captured after living for years under different fictional names. Karadžić had been a Bosnian Serb politician who was believed to be responsible for ordering the Srebrenica massacre.

Another key figure in the Srebrenica massacre was turned over to authorities in May 2011. The former Bosnian Serb military leader Ratko Mladić was captured and put on trial for crimes against humanity.

■ Slobodan Milošević went on trial in 2002.

The slaughter of Srebrenica occurred despite the presence of the United Nations' peacekeeping force. The peacekeeping soldiers were from the Netherlands and did not have a "stake" in the conflict. Because they were not part of any of the ethnic groups, they had no reason to favor one side over the other. So it would seem they would be a perfect choice to keep the peace. Yet they still failed.

Some blame the small size of the force and say they did not have enough weapons. Why do you think they could not stop the slaughter? Do you think a "peacekeeping army" can be successful? Does it make sense to place trained soldiers in a land where they are not fighting for either side in a conflict? How can peacekeepers succeed in protecting the innocent without fighting against an enemy?

AFRICA

On the continent of Africa, political unrest has torn apart several nations in the last half-century, leading to a number of genocides. Just as in other genocides, the roots of these disasters are deep-seated ethnic resentment coming to the surface when national leadership is in turmoil.

Rwanda: Hutu vs. Tutsi

On April 7, 1994, Rwandan president Juvénal Habyarimana was assassinated when his plane was shot out of the sky. This assassination triggered a **coup** by Hutu militia and led directly to genocide.

Historians believe that Hutus and Tutsi people lived in relative peace until Europeans arrived in the 1890s. Germany claimed Rwanda as a colony before control was passed to Belgium after World War I. But from their first contact with Europeans, the relationship between the native Hutus and Tutsis began to change in ways that would have deadly consequences a century later.

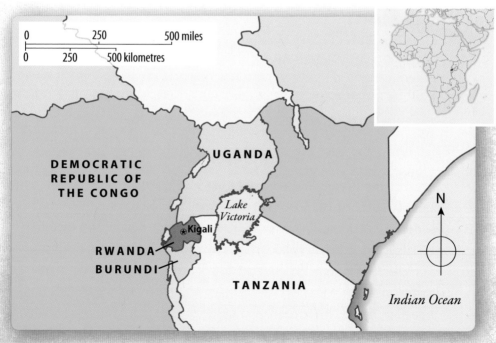

■ Rwanda is a small, landlocked country in Central Africa.

Rwanda was a farm-based society. Tutsis farmed cattle, which put them in a higher social class than Hutus, who worked in farm fields. The two peoples were similar to each other, but the Europeans made a point of distinguishing slight facial or skin differences between the groups. This hatched a division in the minds of the Rwandans. (Again, genocides happen most often in societies where resentments are built up due to even small differences.)

■ These are the grim remains of a massacre during the Rwandan genocide.

The differences exploded in a revolt in the 1950s. The Hutus ejected the Tutsi leaders and eventually killed many thousands of Tutsis in the process. When Rwanda gained its independence as a nation in 1960, the Hutus won control of the new national government. Juvénal Habyarimana was a Hutu, and had ruled Rwanda from 1973 until his assassination in 1994. The exact person responsible for the assassination was never identified, but as soon as the president's plane went down, a Hutu revolt was launched. As the struggle to gain control of the government ensued, a Hutu genocide was unleashed against Tutsis across Rwanda.

The fastest rate of killing ever

The speed with which the Rwandan genocide unfolded was mind boggling. In just 100 days, approximately 800,000 people were massacred. On one day alone, April 20, 1994, about 35,000 to 43,000 people were killed within six hours. Historians believe that Rwandans were killed in this genocide at a rate faster than any other event in human history. Even the Nazis, who had built factories for the single purpose of killing large numbers of people quickly, had never killed at such a ferocious speed.

The swift, brutal, Rwandan genocide took place in broad daylight. Families were dragged out of their homes, tortured, raped, and murdered in the middle of the street. Ordinary citizens took part in the killing. Radio announcers encouraged Hutus to kill Tutsis, neighbor slaughtered neighbor. Hutus who resisted were forced to kill at gunpoint by Hutu militia.

Almost as quickly as it began, the genocide ended. The Tutsi-led Rwandan Patriotic Front (RPF) had been engaged in a military war with the Hutu forces from the day of the president's assassination. The RPF gradually made gains in the war. On the 100th day of the struggle, they overthrew the Hutus, ending the civil war and the genocide at once.

Countries, such as the United Kingdom and the United States, are commonly expected to lend support in other countries' struggles, but often they must step back and allow countries to sort out their own problems. In the case of Rwanda, U.S. President Bill Clinton later realized he should have sent forces to intervene. He later said, "… we in the United States and the world community did not do as much as we could have and should have done to try to limit what occurred."

This is the testimony of Clare, a woman who survived the genocide in Rwanda. Her husband and two children were both killed.

"I was taken captive, and experienced all forms of torture. I was beaten and hit badly. I was forced to drink blood from dead and injured people … With my son, they took us to a pit by a roadside to be killed. We were pushed in alive … After some time I began to feel my senses, and memory, return… And then I remembered my son. But when I reached out to touch him, I could only feel his smashed skull."

The role of outsiders

The powerful nations of the world were not able to do anything to stop the Rwandan genocide. Or, some would say, the world powers chose not to do anything. The United Nations had placed a team in Rwanda before the genocide began. Romeo Dallaire, the general of the United Nations Assistance Mission for Rwanda, had learned that the Hutus were planning a genocide and knew where they were stockpiling their weapons. But when Dallaire reported this information to his superiors at the United Nations, he was told that the United Nations' role was to observe and to assist, not to take action against one side or the other.

■ This photo shows a UN peacekeeper watching over a refugee camp in Rwanda.

DEBATE

When is it appropriate for one nation to step in and intervene in another country's affairs? If a country has the right to govern itself, then should other countries stay out of internal conflicts no matter what is going on?

Darfur

It seems that one of the sad truths about all genocides is that we, as a people, have not learned from the past. We study history, but it quickly seems like ancient history, and then some people think that ancient history will not be repeated. It is difficult to imagine that such an atrocity as genocide could ever happen again. Yet genocides have happened throughout history, and they continue today. Even while the crisis in Rwanda occurred, a nearby civil war was starting to rip apart the giant country of Sudan.

■ Darfur occupies the western part of Sudan.

"We didn't learn anything from the Holocaust and it happened (again) in Rwanda. We didn't learn anything from Rwanda because it's happening in Darfur."

Leo Kabalisa, a Rwandan who escaped before the genocide

When the Darfur genocide began, Sudan was basically divided into three parts. The government and capital city of Khartoum were based in the north, and they relied on the money produced by the oil fields in the southern region. In the south, rebel groups who wanted more control of the country had come into conflict with the north. Darfur lay to the west, populated by farmers and nomads. Civil war had flared between the north and south many times over the years, and Darfur, for a long time, had been unhappy with the support it received from the central government. (In 2011, part of the southern region became an independent country, the Republic of South Sudan.)

There is also a cultural divide in Sudan. In the north, most people are Arab Muslim, while the south is primarily African (non-Arab) Muslim. In Darfur, a mix of ethnicities have lived together uneasily and have come into conflict with each other several times. The mix of political disputes and ethnic resentments have brewed for years, and in 2003, they boiled over.

On April 25, 2003, a squad from Darfur attacked a military base in the north in order to ignite a revolt against the government of Omar al-Bashir. In response, Bashir brought not only his own military, but the Janjaweed as well. The name of this militia group translates as "evil men on horseback." The military and Janjaweed were a well-coordinated death machine. Prior to attacking a Darfur village, the area's mobile phone service would be cut off so the people could not warn others or their defense forces. Next, the military would bomb the village from planes, sometimes using cluster bombs and even chemical weapons. Then the Janjaweed would ride in to wreak further destruction.

Janjaweed militia behaved as wildly and brutally as the Nazi Einsatzgruppen squads that terrorized Eastern European citizens in World War II. Janjaweed squads murdered, raped, and tortured at will. They burned entire villages to the ground. They poured poison into wells so that any survivors could not continue to live there. As with other genocides, it is clear that simple military victory was not the goal. The intention was to crush the very life out of Darfur.

The conflict in Darfur is ongoing. Some peace agreements have been discussed, but none have taken hold. Although the United States helped the north and south negotiate a treaty to end their civil war, the Darfur conflict continues. Not surprisingly, the Sudan government does not admit what other authorities have claimed: that genocide has taken place in Darfur. In 2004, U.S. General Colin Powell called Darfur a genocide. The United Nations estimates that 300,000 people have been killed. Sudanese President Bashir says that only 10,000 have died.

Meanwhile, an angry outcry from human rights groups has called for governments to impose their will and stop the genocide. Pressure has been placed on corporations to stop doing business with the Sudanese government as a way of applying economic pressure. Darfur is top priority for activist groups, and mass protests have been staged in major cities. Celebrities, such as George Clooney and Angelina Jolie, have come forward to educate millions of people about the situation.

TORTURE AND HUMILIATION

The use of rape is a common tool for humiliation and torture in genocides. In Darfur, women and girls were raped repeatedly by the Janjaweed soldiers. Many of these victims then had their hands marked permanently so the entire community would know their shame. In genocide, the goal is not only to kill but to humiliate a group of people and crush their spirit. Why do you think these perpetrators think it's necessary to torture and humiliate their victims? What effect does this have on survivors?

CASE STUDY

Darfur's IDPs

When a natural disaster, war, genocide, or other major disruption strikes, a massive number of people are uprooted from their homes. Some become refugees and resettle in another place. In Darfur, about 250,000 refugees have resettled, mostly in the neighboring country of Chad. Others, however, have nowhere to go. For various reasons, they cannot relocate to a safe new home, so they become Internally Displaced Persons, or IDPs.

It is estimated that the Darfur conflict has created 2.7 million IDPs who live in camps and rely entirely on aid organizations for shelter, health care, food, and clothing. The Sudanese government has inflicted its will further on the Darfur people by interfering with aid organizations' ability to bring supplies to the IDPs. Sudan has blocked supply lines and stopped relief agencies from entering the country. Those aid workers who do manage to get into Darfur say they are threatened with violence and kidnapping.

■ These people have been displaced by the Darfur genocide.

Why do you think the United Nations or world powers are unable to stop Sudan from interfering with aid for IDPs? What do you think Sudan has to gain by interfering with aid for the IDPs?

MEMORY AND HEALING

"Never shall I forget that night, the first night in camp, which has turned my life into one long night, seven times cursed and seven times sealed."

These words are from *Night*, a book by Elie Wiesel, an award-winning author. It tells the story of his journey as a prisoner through four Nazi concentration camps as a teenage boy. Wiesel later won the Nobel Peace Prize, which is awarded to honor accomplishments that have benefited humankind in some way. In his many writing and speaking appearances, he has repeated the message that memory is an essential component in preventing other genocides from happening. Humans must learn the truth of what happened in concentration camps, we must hear the testimonies of people who saw their relatives shot like animals and thrown into pits, and we must also hear the explanations and confessions of the criminals who committed these acts.

Memorials and museums

It has always been a tradition to build statues and other structures to remember wars and fallen soldiers. As we have begun to confront genocide in the last century, we have created ways of acknowledging and remembering genocide victims in a public way, too. Here are some examples:

- Hundreds of Holocaust memorials and museums have been built in many places around the world, from Jerusalem to the United Kingdom.

- In Germany and Poland, actual sites of Nazi crimes have been turned into memorials and museums. For instance, visitors can now walk through original buildings that still stand at Auschwitz.

- In Yerevan, Armenia, the memorial Tsitsernakaberd is a 145-foot- (44-meter-) long stele (funeral stone) that rises out of the ground to represent the rebirth of Armenia following its near destruction at the hands of the Turks.

■ The Hall of Names at Yad Vashem, the memorial museum in Israel, displays hundreds of photographs of people who perished in the Holocaust.

- In Phnom Penh, Cambodia, the Tuol Sleng prison has been turned into a memorial museum.

- In 2003, the Bosnian government opened a memorial cemetery in Srebrenica in honor of the victims who died in the genocide there. The vast field is dotted with thousands of rows of white gravestones, creating a frightening reminder of just how many people were killed there.

- In Kigali, Rwanda, the Kigali Memorial Center was opened on the site of the murder of more than 250,000 people. In addition to a museum and visitors' center, the site includes several mass graves where bodies that were originally discarded into pits have been buried with care and dignity.

Education

Most genocide memorial museums include an education component that provides books, documents, photos, and films to show younger generations the truth about genocide. Many schools require that genocide is studied as part of a social studies curriculum.

To help preserve the memories of witnesses, organizations have launched oral history projects in which witnesses are interviewed so that their testimonies can be documented permanently. The film director Steven Spielberg launched the Survivors of the Shoah Visual History Foundation in 1994, which captured nearly 52,000 witness testimonies. The collection is now part of a larger program that records oral histories on the genocides in Armenia, Cambodia, and Rwanda.

Closure

Our memory of genocides would be incomplete, however, if the story were told only by the victims. Governments strive to capture, try, and punish genocide criminals for two reasons. First, they want justice to be served. Second, we need to hear the perpetrators' testimonies (and confessions, if they give any) so that we can have a complete truth. We need to affirm that the crimes were committed by people—real people just like us.

Trials for genocides from both the recent and distant past are still ongoing, In 2011, four key Khmer Rouge leaders were scheduled to go on trial for their actions in the Cambodian genocide, which had ended 32 years earlier. Not all trials are held in traditional courtrooms. In Rwandan cities and villages, about 10,000 *gacaca* courts were established in the years following the genocide. These courts were informal gatherings at parks or other outdoor spaces. The purpose was to listen and discuss, not to punish. Judges of *gacaca* courts were respected people in the community—both Tutsis and Hutus. This was a way that people found to bring a sense of closure to the past, and perhaps live and work alongside former enemies.

DEBATE

When we learn that many acts of genocide are carried out by ordinary human beings, we realize that humans are capable of immense good but also incredible evil. Do you think that any person is capable of murder? Do you think that any society—including our own contemporary society—is capable of genocide?

■ At a Rwandan reconciliation program, children enjoy the simple pleasures of peace.

Although just about all perpetrators of the Nazi Holocaust have died of old age, international lawyers are still filing lawsuits against present-day companies that helped the Nazis in the past. The lawsuits ask for restitution—money to be paid to organizations that represent survivors' families. For instance, the giant German bank, Deutsche Bank, was discovered to have helped fund the Nazis' construction of Auschwitz.

Another form of restitution is tracking down the possessions that Nazis stole and returning them to survivors' families. At least $10 billion in money, property, jewelry, and other objects fell into the hands of the Nazis. In recent years, it was discovered that certain works of art in museums had actually been stolen from wealthy Jews' collections by the Nazis. International courts ordered the works to be returned to the surviving family members.

These efforts are meant to bring closure—a sense of settling old disputes, a sense of having some bit of justice served. But closure must not be taken to mean forgetting. It has become all too easy to assume that, if truth is spoken and criminals are punished, a crime can be locked away and forgotten. Humanity's worst crimes must be kept out in the open and observed. If not, they will surely be repeated.

TIMELINE OF MAJOR GENOCIDES

Not all historians agree on which events qualify as genocides and which are other types of tragedies. This timeline includes events that most experts agree were genocides; other events in history may also have been genocides.

Date	Genocide
149–146 BCE	Destruction of Carthage – Roman soldiers kill 250,000 Carthaginians
1095–1200s CE	The Crusades (see pages 6–7)
1206–1368	The Mongol Conquests (see pages 8–9)
1400s–1700s	Spanish Inquisition (see page 8)
1794	War in the Vendée – French soldiers kill approximately 170,000 French peasants
1830s	Trail of Tears (see page 11)
1860s	Circassian War – Russia kills at least 1 million Circassians and forces 500,000 more out of the region
1828–1832	Black War of Australia – Actions by British colonists lead to the deaths of nearly 2,000 Tasmanian Aborigines (original people)
1845–1852	Great Famine of Ireland – About 25 percent of the Irish population die of starvation due to British control of crops
1915–1918	Armenian Genocide (see pages 12–17)
1932–1933	Stalin's Forced Famine (see page 23)
1937–1938	Nanjing Massacre – Japan's capture of the Chinese city leads to an estimated 100,000–300,000 deaths
1938–1945	German Holocaust (see pages 18–31)
1947	Partition of India – more than 500,000 deaths when the country is divided
1975–1979	Cambodian Genocide (see pages 32–37)
1988	Saddam Hussein's attack on the Kurds – more than 2 million deaths
1992–1995	Bosnian Genocide (see pages 38–45)
1994	Rwanda (see pages 46–49)
2003–present	Darfur (see pages 50–53)

CHARACTERISTICS OF GENOCIDE

Not every genocide unfolds in exactly the same manner, but historians note that most genocides include many of the following characteristics.

Separation
Ethnic, racial, or religious groups are separated from the larger society by labeling and name-calling.

Changed identity
Through forced religious conversion or change of citizenship, the group's identity is changed.

Starvation
Food supplies are controlled, leading to famine.

Dehumanization
Through propaganda, a group is characterized as alien, diseased, or non-human ("devils," "rats," "insects," etc.).

Erased cultural history
The culture and memory of the people is attacked through the destruction of libraries, museums, documents, churches, and other buildings.

Removal of children
The minority group's children are taken away from their parents. This is an attempt to end the cultural group by erasing its youngest generation.

Birth control
Adults are sterilized so they cannot have babies and a new generation cannot be born.

GENOCIDE

Torture
People are tortured for no reason at all; sometimes they are allowed to live, and sometimes the torture ends with their murder.

Legal and economic restrictions
Laws are passed that deprive people of legal rights, as well as jobs, income, healthcare, and housing.

Mass murder
All genocides are marked by the murder of large numbers of people.

Deportation
A large portion of the population is moved out of the region—either to another state or country, or to internment camps or concentration camps (prisons).

Planning
Genocides do not happen by accident. Ruling groups make conscious, specific plans for how to carry out the genocide.

Humiliation
Both through propaganda and violence carried out in public, the minority group is shamed and humiliated (they are beaten in front of mocking crowds; they are stripped of clothing; women and girls are raped).

GLOSSARY

Allies alliance of nations that fought the Axis powers in World War II, including Britain, the United States, and the Soviet Union

anti-Semitic prejudiced against Jews

Aryan term used by the Nazis to describe an ethnic group of white Europeans that was supposed to be superior to other ethnic groups

atrocity terrible, unimaginable crime

Axis alliance of nations that fought the Allies in World War II, including Nazi Germany, Italy, and Japan

chemical weapon bomb that releases deadly gases into the air

communist supporter of communism, which is a system of government that does not allow idividuals the right to own property, and rejects classes in society

concentration camp prison where large groups of people are taken

convert to alter; to change from one religion to another

coup struggle within a government in which its leader is removed from power

death camp place where prisoners are taken to be murdered in mass numbers

democracy system of government built on individual liberties and a government that represents citizens

deportation forceful removal of people from the place where they live

displacement moving a group of people out of their homes by force

Einsatzgruppen "death squads"; groups of Nazi soldiers who committed mass killings during the Holocaust

ethnic referring to the culture, race, language, homeland, or religion that binds a group together

ethnic cleansing expulsion or killing of an ethnic group or groups from a society or region

execute put to death

expel force someone to leave a place, especially a country

exterminate get rid of, completely and permanently

famine mass starvation

heretic person who is thought of as wrong for disagreeing with the teachings of a certain religion

human rights basic rights to life and freedom which all people are born with

inquisition official investigation or trial

intellectual person who is devoted to thought and analysis

internment camp place where displaced people are held, usually by force

massacre murder of a large number of people

militia group of citizens who act as an army but are not part of a country's actual army

persecute mistreat; make into a victim

propaganda misinformation; news stories, pictures, movies, and other media messages that are false or misleading

Soviet Union 20th-century communist country of which today's Russia was a major part

tribunal court with a judge

United Nations international organization comprised of many nations that enforces international law and provides aid to people and nations in need

FURTHER INFORMATION

Books

Nonfiction

Filipovic, Zlata. *Zlata's Diary: A Child's Life in Wartime Sarajevo.* Logan, Iowa: Perfection Learning, 2006.

Frank, Anne. *The Diary of a Young Girl.* New York: Bantam Books, 1993.

Keat, Nawuth and Martha E. Kendall.. *Alive in the Killing Fields: Surviving the Khmer Rouge Genocide.* Des Moines, Iowa: National Geographic, 2009.

Kherdian, David. *The Road from Home: A True Story of Courage, Survival, and Hope.* New York: Greenwillow Books, 1995.

Fiction

Lowry, Lois. *Number the Stars.* Boston: Sandpiper, 2011.

Wiesel, Elie. *Night.* New York: Hill and Wang, 2008.

Websites

Darfur Photo Essay
www.unicef.org/photoessays/25400.html
A photo essay by UNICEF that explores the daily life of Darfur survivors and refugees.

Kigali Memorial Center
www.kigalimemorialcentre.org/old/index.html
The website for the Rwanda memorial cemetery includes web resources on the genocide and its aftermath.

Nicole's Journey
www.learngenocide.com
Experience the interactive journey of Nicole, an Armenian American trying to track her family's roots through the Armenian Genocide.

United Nations

www.un.org/en/preventgenocide/adviser/index.shtml

The United Nations website includes information on its efforts to prevent genocide.

USC Shoah Foundation Institute

college.usc.edu/vhi

Website home to tens of thousands of video testimonies by witnesses to the Holocaust and the genocides of Armenia, Cambodia, and Rwanda.

Guide to genocide museums

Here is a selective guide to some of the world's main museums devoted to remembering genocide and educating the public about these events. Each museum's website includes a virtual tour of its exhibits.

Armenian Genocide Museum

Tsitsernakaberd Memorial Complex

RA, Armenia Yerevan 0028

www.genocide-museum.am/eng/index.php

Museum of Genocide Victims

Aukų str. 2A

LT-01113 Vilnius, Lithuania

www.genocid.lt/muziejus/en

The United States Holocaust Memorial Museum

100 Raoul Wallenberg Place, SW

Washington, D.C. 20024-2126

(202) 488-0400

www.ushmm.org

Yad Vashem

The Holocaust Martyrs' and Heroes' Remembrance Authority

Har Hazikaron

P.O. Box 3477

Jerusalem 91034 Israel

www.yadvashem.org

INDEX